LEGENDS OF CHIMA™
POWER UP!

Written by Julia March

Written by Julia March
Editors Pamela Afram, Gaurav Joshi
Art Editors Jo Connor, Karan Chaudhary
Managing Editors Simon Hugo,
Chitra Subramanyam
Managing Art Editors Ron Stobbart, Neha Ahuja
Art Director Lisa Lanzarini
DTP Designers Umesh Singh Rawat, Rajdeep Singh
Pre-Production Producer Marc Staples
Pre-Production Manager Sunil Sharma
Producer Louise Daly
Reading Consultant Linda B. Gambrell, Ph.D.

Publisher Julie Ferris
Publishing Director Simon Beecroft

First published in the United States in 2015 by DK Publishing
345 Hudson Street, New York, New York 10014

Copyright © 2015 Dorling Kindersley Limited
A Penguin Random House Company
10 9 8 7 6 5 4 3 2 1
001–273368–Jan/15

A CIP catalogue record for this book is
available from the Library of Congress.

ISBN: 978-1-4654-2949-0 (Hardback)
ISBN: 978-1-4654-2950-6 (Paperback)

Color reproduction by Alta Image Ltd. UK
Printed and bound in China by South China Printing Co. Ltd.

www.LEGO.com
www.dk.com

A WORLD OF IDEAS:
SEE ALL THERE IS TO KNOW

Contents

Welcome to Chima™!

The land of Chima™ is a magical world rich in a potent energy source called CHI. It flows down from a floating mountain called Mount Cavora, into the Sacred Pool. There, the liquid CHI turns into glowing orbs.

Thousands of years ago, some of Chima's animals dared to drink the liquid CHI from the Sacred Pool.

Amazing things happened! They began to walk on two legs, to talk like humans, and to build and invent things.

Today, the animal tribes of Chima use CHI orbs to power up their vehicles, their weapons, and themselves.

Tribes of Chima

Not so long ago, the tribes of Chima went to war over CHI. Now they share it fairly, and Chima is at peace.

Every animal tribe has its own hero. Laval is a young prince who will one day lead the brave and noble Lions. Worris mainly hangs out with his own tribe, the down-to-earth Wolves.

Razar is a typical Raven—always out to make a profit, even if it means swindling his friends. Eris loves to think and dream, like all the Eagles. Cragger the Crocodile was once greedy for CHI. He caused a lot of trouble, but he has learned his lesson. As for Gorzan the Gorilla, he just wants to relax and enjoy the flowers!

Power-up Moment

To reach their full warrior strength, every hero must power up with CHI. It is a thrilling sight to see an animal power up! They plug a CHI orb into their harness. A great surge of energy fills them as they connect to the pure power of their tribe. Then their "inner warrior" appears. This giant figure glows blue if the animal wants to do good and red if it wants to do bad. Laval's inner warrior glows blue because he wants to help Chima.

The power-up moment only lasts a few seconds, but it brings extra strength that lasts for many hours.

HOW DOES IT FEEL TO POWER UP?

I'm bursting with energy. It makes me want to howl! Arroooo!

I feel so strong,
I could fight all my
enemies at once...
and beat them!

Guardians of CHI

The Lions are the oldest and wisest tribe. They guard the Sacred Pool, where the CHI orbs form. The Sacred Pool is in the Lion Temple, at the center of Lion City.

The Lions divide the CHI orbs fairly between the tribes. They are careful to take just the right amount of CHI from the Sacred Pool. If they took too much or too little, Chima would be thrown out of balance. Bad things would happen. There might be floods, earthquakes, and other disasters too horrible to think about! That is why the Lions take their role very seriously.

RULES OF CHI

Hi kids—it's Cragger! Here are the rules of CHI. Please stick to them. I broke them once, and it ended up with everyone fighting. Don't make the same mistake!

DO THIS!

- Do use CHI only for good. Heed the Lions' warning: "Use it well, use it wisely."

- Do use your CHI sparingly. Remember, it has to last you a whole month.

- Do guard your CHI well. Thieves might be around!

DON'T DO THIS!

- Don't use CHI before you are old enough. Your tribe leader knows when you are ready.

- Don't try to take more than your fair share of CHI.

- Don't try to store up too much CHI. Use your monthly share, or Chima will become unbalanced.

Powering Up Vehicles

The animals' battle vehicles must be powered up with CHI in order to run. To power up a vehicle, you have to fit CHI orbs into special plugs on it.

Can you see the CHI orb plugged into Equila's Eagle Striker? There should be a second orb on the other side, but a thief has stolen it!

Equila and Eglor will have to chase the thief and get it back. Luckily, there is enough CHI in the Striker to keep it going for a long time. Blue CHI flows through the tubes on each side, to power the twin rocket shooters.

GORZAN'S
GORILLA STRIKER
MIGHTY MECH

Gorzan's Gorilla Striker is a big, mean, banana-shooting machine! Foes fast enough to dodge its swinging arms might still be hit by a well-aimed banana. Ouch!

JOINTED FINGERS
Strong, jointed fingers are ideal for scooping up enemy weapons—or the enemies themselves.

CHI TUBES
CHI flows through tubes to power the hands. Hands this big use up a lot of CHI!

STOMPING FEET
Heavy feet are good for stomping through thick jungle. They squash prickly plants flat.

BANANA SHOOTER

The Shooter fires bananas one after another. Unripe bananas can knock foes off their feet.

CHI PLUG

A blue CHI orb is plugged into the Gorilla Striker's chest. Above it are six blue missiles.

19

Powering Up Speedorz

Speedorz are small, fast chariots. The animals of Chima use them for battle, for racing at the Grand Arena, or just for fun.

Speedor wheels are carved from rocks that fell from Mount Cavora long ago. The wheels draw their power directly from nature. Because of this, you do not have to plug in a CHI orb to power up a Speedor. Instead, you must ride it through a lush part of the jungle. Dry or stony areas are no good for powering up Speedorz, so if your Speedor power runs out in a desert, you might be in trouble!

Going for Gold

Golden CHI is much rarer than blue
CHI. Just one orb of it is harvested
from the Sacred Pool each month. You
cannot power up with Golden CHI, but
it has another valuable quality. It can
be used to transform landscapes in an
instant. This is called "terraforming."

Everyone wants an orb of Golden CHI, but the only way to get one is by winning a Speedor race at Chima's Grand Arena. These monthly contests are for the bravest and most skilled Speedor riders only. The winner takes home a precious Golden CHI orb and is hailed as a hero by their tribe.

Battle Ready!

Armor protects warriors in battle, and its color shows which tribe they are from. It features tribal symbols too, like the Lion faces on Laval's knee pads and belt. On the armor's chest plate there is a plug for a CHI orb. When a warrior powers-up, his or her weapons become powered-up, too. Every hero in Chima has a favorite weapon. For Laval, it is his mighty Shado Valious.

Cragger trusts in his sharp-toothed Royal Vengious. Eris has her light-as-air Halor, while Gorzan loves his amazing Banana Buster.

The Phoenix Tribe

The Phoenix are an ancient tribe who possess a powerful form of CHI called Fire CHI. For a long time the Phoenix have hidden away on Mount Cavora. Now that Chima is in danger, they have revealed themselves to the other tribes.

The Phoenix are ready to share their Fire CHI with the other tribes to help them save Chima. But those who want to use it must pass a special test first. Fire CHI is very dangerous!

King Fluminox is the Phoenix leader. He is very serious. He wishes his son, Flinx, would grow up. Flinx seems to want to be a child forever.

He has still not grown fire wings like the other Phoenix.

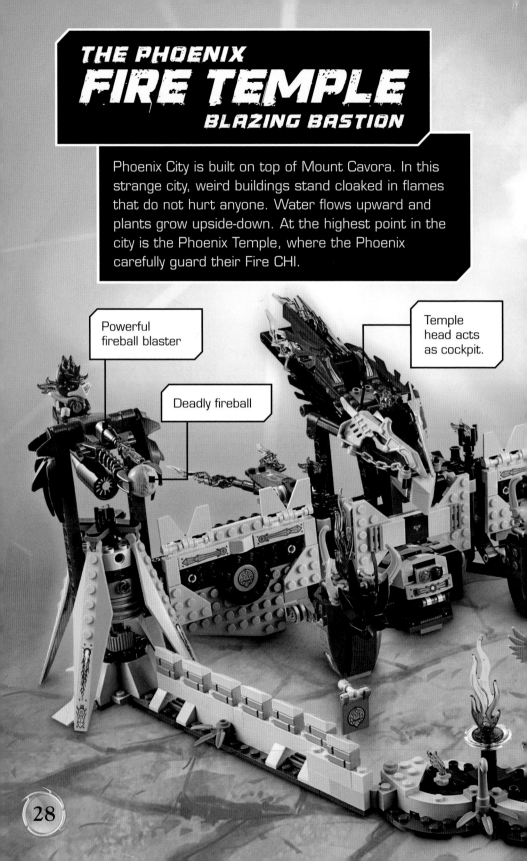

THE PHOENIX
FIRE TEMPLE
BLAZING BASTION

Phoenix City is built on top of Mount Cavora. In this strange city, weird buildings stand cloaked in flames that do not hurt anyone. Water flows upward and plants grow upside-down. At the highest point in the city is the Phoenix Temple, where the Phoenix carefully guard their Fire CHI.

Powerful fireball blaster

Deadly fireball

Temple head acts as cockpit.

Phoenix guard watches from above.

Foltrax is an ace pilot.

Blazing Bastion

The Fire Temple has many levels. The most amazing of all is the uppermost level, called the Blazing Bastion. It can detach from the Temple to become a massive jet fighter armed with Flame Pulsorz. King Fluminox does not like traveling in the Blazing Bastion, because he hates flying!

Torch holders become talons in flight.

Walls fold back to form wings.

Entry restricted to a select few

Fire Power

Fire CHI is dangerous. Only special heroes like Cragger and his friends are allowed to power up with it. A Fire CHI power-up is even more awesome than a regular power-up.

When Cragger plugs an orb of Fire CHI into his harness, his inner warrior appears in a burst of roaring flames. A fiery glow called the Power Warrior Glow surrounds him. Cragger has become a Fire CHI Warrior!

While the power-up lasts, Cragger is protected against burns. Any weapons he uses will shoot flames or cause heat explosions. Best of all, he is immune to the Freeze Powers of an icy army that is invading Chima.

31

Fire Tribes

The Tigers are the loyal guards of the Phoenix. Because they possess Fire CHI, these two tribes are known as the Fire Tribes.

The Tiger leader is named Tormak. He is very wise. King Fluminox always consults him before making a decision.

The Tiger Tribe is not just for tigers. Tormak has allowed some other big cats to join. They include Lundor, a leopard, and Li'Ella, a female lion. Tormak has adopted Li'Ella as his daughter. When the heroes first arrive in Phoenix City to try the Fire CHI, Li'Ella is excited to meet Laval. She has never seen another lion before!

Threat to Chima

For many years, a tribe of Saber-Tooth Tigers slept, frozen in ice. Then a stray orb of CHI woke them up. Now they are on the march, freezing everything in Chima with their Freeze Powers. Plants become icicles and animals are trapped in blocks of ice.

These fierce warriors are led by the cruel, white-furred Sir Fangar. His base is an Ice Fort on a glacier that is slowly gliding across Chima.

Sir Fangar wants to turn Chima into an icy wasteland and collect frozen animals as trophies. He also wants to make Li'Ella his queen.

Hunter Tribes

The Saber-Tooth Tigers have used CHI to wake up other bad tribes. They are the big, lumbering Mammoths, the cunning, lazy Vultures, and the vicious Ice Bears. Together, these tribes are known as the Hunters. With their ragged, holey skins and glowing bones, they look scary and horrible.

The Hunters use blue CHI in a different way from the other tribes. Plugging an orb into their harness only keeps them awake. To power up, they must also eat an orb.

Only one thing scares the Hunters—Fire CHI! It can scorch them badly and take their Freeze Powers away.

Freeze Powers

The Hunters' bodies give out Freeze Powers that turn nearby objects to ice. To freeze things further away, they use weapons called Ice Pulsorz. They freeze trees, clouds, animals, and even Pulse Beams from their enemies' weapons.

The Hunters freeze Laval, Cragger, Eris, Razar, Worris, and Gorzan as well. If the heroes power-up quickly, they can break out of the ice before it gets solid. But when they do, the Hunters just freeze them again! They need something to make them immune from Freeze Powers.

They need Fire CHI.

SIR FANGAR'S
EVIL PLAN

Greetings, fans. How am I conquering Chima? One battle at a time! Want to see my standard battle plan? Of course you do! Read and learn...

1

AIR ATTACK

First, I will send up Vardy's Ice Vulture Glider to spot where the enemy is hiding.

2

GROUND ATTACK

Then I ride in on my Saber-Tooth Walker. I will fire my ice-tipped missiles and freeze every animal I can find.

3
MAMMOTH ASSAULT

It's time to bring in Maula's Mammoth Stomper. We pop the frozen animals into the Stomper's prison and bring them to my Ice Fort museum.

4
FINAL GOAL

Every day my glacier moves further across Chima. Soon we will reach Mount Cavora. Then, my friends, we will have the Phoenix in our icy grasp. Onward!

GET READY TO FEEL THE CHILL, TRIBES OF CHIMA!

Trial by Fire

Fire CHI can burn anyone who is not
smart and brave enough to use it.
The Phoenix set the heroes a scary
test called a "Trial by Fire" to find
out if they are worthy.

In the test, Laval and Cragger have
to balance above a pit of flames.

Cragger's tail catches on fire, but they still pass. Afterwards, Laval, Cragger, and Eris are given special flame-red fire suits to show that they are allowed to use Fire CHI. Later on, Razar, Worris, and Gorzan receive fire suits too. They all get new gold armor with a special plug for Fire CHI.

Fire vs. Ice

Oh, no! Gorzan has become separated from his friends, and Sir Fangar is charging toward him in his Saber-Tooth Walker. Gorzan can see the Saber-Tooth Walker's crunching teeth and icicle claws as it gets closer and closer. He can hear its ice-tipped missiles as they whistle through the air!

The Gorilla tribe hero powers up with Fire CHI just in time. He grabs his red-hot Blayzhammer and whirls it around. Sir Fangar does not dare to come any closer in case he gets scorched. Now Gorzan can escape with his blue CHI.

CHOOSE YOUR CH

BLUE CHI

CONSTANT SUPPLY
There is a steady supply of blue CHI, so it is perfect for your regular, everyday power-ups.

SAFE AND RELIABL
When in doubt, stick w what you know. With blue CHI, you are muc less likely to mess up.

DOUBLE DOSE
Are you a Hunter? Then you can only use blue CHI. But remember, you always need two orbs.

CHI is much stronger than blue CHI. That
[does] not mean it is always the best kind to
[u]se. Often, good old blue CHI is best. And
[some]times you may not have a choice at all!

FIRE CHI

LIMITED ACCESS
You can only get Fire
CHI from the Phoenix.
They might decide not to
give you any.

HOT TO HANDLE
This CHI burns! Take
care using it, or you
might hurt your friends
[in]stead of your enemies.

ANTI FREEZE
It makes you immune to
freezing, so it is ideal for
fighting the Hunters. If you
are a Hunter… forget it!

Fire CHI Speedorz

When warriors power up with Fire CHI, their Speedorz become powered up too. They are transformed into Fire Speedorz. As soon as the warrior jumps into his or her Speedor, it grows big, powerful wings or claws made of fire. Like normal weapons, these wings or claws can jab, slash, push, and bash.

But because they are fiery, they can also melt a Hunter's icy weapons and vehicles.

Sir Fangar thinks he is a master of the ice, but jousting with Laval might be a mistake. One touch from the fiery claws on Laval's Fire CHI Speedor and Sir Fangar might end up sitting in a puddle instead of a Speedor!

Fire Vehicles

When a warrior plugs a Fire CHI orb into a tank, truck, or airplane, it instantly transforms into a Fire Vehicle.

The vehicle quickly expands up to three times its normal size. It rears up like a giant, angry beast, and begins to glow. Flames may shoot from its mouth like fiery breath. They may sprout from its back like red-hot wings, or crackle from the tips of its claws.

Laval's Fire Lion is an awesome sight when it is powered up with Fire CHI. It looks like a lion ready to pounce. But unlike a real lion, this one has claws of burning fire!

Me and the Mammoth, right before my winning blow!

King Lagravis,
The Lion Temple,
Chima

Dear Father,

We had the scariest battle with the
Hunters today... and we won!
Dad, you would be proud of me.

The Hunters took us by surprise, so we
had to power up with Fire CHI fast. They
fired freeze blasts at us, so we grabbed our
Pulsorz and started melting them. But they
kept coming.

The scariest part was when they got really
close. This huge Mammoth charged at me,
but I stood my ground and fought him with
Fire CHI. Eris and the others fought like
crazy, too. Flames were everywhere! Then the
Hunters just ran away. Dad, it was great!

Your loving son,
Laval

Fire Harness Quest

Fire CHI is very strong, but so are the Hunters' Freeze Powers. The Hunters' glacier has reached the middle of Chima. Soon, ice will cover the land. There is just one hope left. Somewhere in Chima, eight magic fire wing harnesses are hidden. They have the power to return Chima to how it was before the Hunters came.

But where is the map that shows where the harnesses are hidden? Tormak has run away with it after an accident charred his fur and turned him into a panther.

The Ultimate Phoenix

The harnesses are found! The heroes
put them on and fly toward
Mount Cavora, willing to give
up their lives to save Chima.
But they do not have to risk their lives.
When they reach Mount Cavora,
Flinx, the little Phoenix prince, is
suddenly transformed into the Ultimate
Phoenix. As he streaks across the sky,
magical Phoenix Fire is unleashed.

The Phoenix Fire covers all
of Chima, melting the ice and
thawing out all the frozen animals.
The Hunters are beaten!

Quiz

1. Where is Phoenix City?

2. Who is the leader of the Saber-Tooth Tiger tribe?

3. What are the three kinds of CHI?

4. What kind of animal is Li'Ella?

5. How do the Hunters power up?

6. Who is the son of King Fluminox?

7. What weapon is this?

8. Which part of the Phoenix Temple turns into a jet?

9. What color armor do the heroes wear with their fire suits?

10. Which weapons fire beams that can freeze things?

Answers on page 61

Glossary

Ancestors
Your relatives from long ago.

Charred
Partly burned by fire.

Expands
Gets bigger.

Harness
Straps you wear that attach you to something.

Immune
Not able to be harmed by something.

Lumbering
Slow and heavy.

Panther
A type of big cat with black fur.

Symbols
Pictures used in place of words.

Trophies
Objects kept by the winner of a contest to remind them of their victory.

Vicious
Fierce and dangerous.

Wasteland
A place where nothing grows and nobody wants to live.

Index

Answers to the quiz on pages 58 and 59:
1. Mount Cavora 2. Sir Fangar 3. Blue, Golden, and Fire
4. Lion 5. By eating an orb of blue CHI
6. Flinx 7. Blayzhammer 8. Blazing Bastion
9. Gold 10. Ice Pulsorz

Guide for Parents

DK Readers is a four-level interactive reading adventure series for children, developing the habit of reading widely for both pleasure and information. These books have an exciting main narrative interspersed with a range of reading genres to suit your child's reading ability, as required by the Common Core State Standards. Each book is designed to develop your child's reading skills, fluency, grammar awareness, and comprehension in order to build confidence and engagement when reading.

Ready for a Reading Alone book
YOUR CHILD SHOULD

- be able to read most words without needing to stop and break them down into sound parts.
- read smoothly, in phrases and with expression.
  By this level, your child will be mostly reading silently.
- self-correct when some word or sentence doesn't sound right.

A Valuable And Shared Reading Experience

For some children, text reading, particularly non-fiction, requires much effort, but adult participation can make this both fun and easier. So here are a few tips on how to use this book with your child.

TIP 1 Check out the contents together before your child begins:

- invite your child to check the blurb, contents page, and layout of the book and comment on it.
- ask your child to make predictions about the story.
- talk about the information your child might want to find out.

TIP 2 Encourage fluent and flexible reading:

- support your child to read in fluent, expressive phrases, making full use of punctuation and thinking about the meaning.

- encourage your child to slow down and check information where appropriate.

TIP 3 Indicators that your child is reading for meaning:

- your child will be responding to the text if he/she is self-correcting and varying his/her voice.
- your child will want to talk about what he/she is reading or is eager to turn the page to find out what will happen next.

TIP 4 Share and discuss:

- encourage your child to recall specific details after each chapter.
- provide opportunities for your child to pick out interesting words and discuss what they mean.
- discuss how the author captures the reader's interest, or how effective the non-fiction layouts are.
- ask questions about the text. These help to develop comprehension skills and awareness of the language used.

A FEW ADDITIONAL TIPS

- read to your child regularly to demonstrate fluency, phrasing, and expression; to find out or check information; and for sharing enjoyment.
- Encourage your child to reread favorite texts to increase reading confidence and fluency.
- Check that your child is reading a range of different types of material, such as poems, jokes, and following instructions.

Series consultant, **Dr. Linda Gambrell**, distinguished Professor of Education at Clemson University, has served as President of the National reading Conference, the College reading Association, and the international reading Association. She is also reading consultant for the **DK Adventures**.

Have you read these other great books from DK?

Join David on an amazing trip to meet elephants in Asia and Africa.

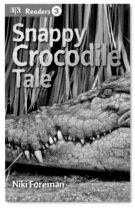

Follow Chris Croc's adventures from a baby to a mighty king of the river.

Enjoy a summer in Heartlake City with Stephanie and friends.

Jump into battle with the animal tribes as they fight to win CHI.

Join Luke Skywalker as he helps the rebels defeat the Empire.

Meet the heroes of Chima™ and help them find the Legend Beasts.

© 2015 Lucasfilm Ltd and TM.